Superlatives from Heaven

Inspiration
for Selfless Service

If you purchased
or acquired this book,
it is because
there is something in this book
to refresh your spirit,
enlighten your soul,
and propel you further
into your destiny.

Superlatives from Heaven

Inspiration
for Selfless Service

by

Starr Parker

Superlatives From Heaven
Volume I, Edition I

Copyright © 2017 Starr Parker

For ordering, booking, permission, questions, or interviews, contact the author, Starr Parker, President of Global Parallel Ministries, Inc. at:
Starr@global parallel.com

Printed in the United States of America
Create Space Publishing

ISBN: 978-0 -9995374-1-1
First Printing 2017

Cover Design: Terena Ribeiro

DEDICATION

To the Father, the Son, Yeshua Ha-Mashiach,
and the Holy Spirit

FOREWORD

Many Americans talk about traveling to Haiti and other places to help the poor, and I am very thankful for those who have been true to their commitments over the years. Starr Parker is one of them. I have known Starr for over a decade, and he has supported the poor in Haiti in so many ways that I will not attempt to list them here. Let me just say that Starr has sacrificed a lot to help the kids in Haiti live better, more promising lives. He is truly my brother in Christ for life.

With love in Christ,

Pastor Guerry LeFranc
Zamar Ministries, Haiti

ACKNOWLEDGMENTS

Ruby Parker for your many sacrifices,
unfailing love and support.

To all who believe
that it is never too late
to make a difference
in the lives of the less fortunate.

The most compassionate person wears no shoes because he is standing in yours.

Rarely can one
show compassion
without being
inconvenienced.

The wealthiest
person on earth is
the one who invests
all his living in
selfless service to
those who are
the least fortunate.

How much of what
you do each day is
about selfless
service to others?

Money comes and
goes, but souls
are eternal.

Lifting souls out

of agony and
despair is the

most profitable

investment we
can make.

THE MOST
CONTENT PERSON
IS THE ONE
WHO IS THE
LEAST CONTENT
WITH WHAT HE HAS
ACCOMPLISHED
SO FAR.

IF YOU'RE
SATISFIED WITH
WHAT YOU'VE
ACCOMPLISHED
SO FAR, MOST
LIKELY, YOU'VE
HARDLY BEGUN.

How different would your life be if you took more time to polish the pearls of hope and gems of potential God placed in your path?

True "saints" may
be born thinking
only of themselves,
but they die
thinking only
of others.

The most beautiful
person in Heaven
is the one who
helped the most
people on earth to
see the beauty
God placed
within them.

Who woke up
this morning
<u>knowing</u> that
she is beautiful
because you
took the time
to be kind?

The most fulfilled people are those who weep alongside the hurting, comfort the broken, and lift the downtrodden.

How many hands
would you need
to count the
number of people
you've comforted
in the last 24 hours?

The richest person
on earth is the one
who selflessly
assigns the least
value to
himself and the
most value
to others.

To God, every human
being is priceless.

How much value do you
give the "least of these"
around you?

The greatest
steward on earth
is the one who divests
all that she has
into the largest number
of people
who cannot possibly
repay her.

When you stand
before the
pearly gates,
it will not matter
who owed
you or how much
you were owed,
but rather how much
you gave in selfless
service to others.

The healthiest
person in Heaven
is the person who
served others on
earth despite
having the
greatest disability.

How do you use
your strengths to
help those who are
vulnerable and
cannot help
themselves?

The sickest person on earth is the person most willing to steal from the most vulnerable to embellish his lifestyle.

Those who are
healthiest among us
live their lives
helping the sick get
well, not prolonging
their plight
for financial gain.

The person that is
the least appealing
is the one
who sees beauty only
in herself.

Did you notice the
beauty in the last
stranger that walked
past you?

The Creator did.

Would you have to
change anything
about yourself to see
total strangers
through eyes
of love?

The greatest error
in life is dying
without having
realized the value of
confession and
repentance.

If confession and
repentance were
beauty products,
how often
do you think
you would use them?

Confession and
repentance are
beauty products for
the daily cleansing of
the soul.

The best friend in life
is the one
so supportive
<u>in times of trouble</u>
that they become
the most
(lovingly) annoying!!!

How far does your
love go for those
<u>you know</u>
that are going
through hardship?

What about those
who you do
<u>not</u> know?

The worst

so-called "success"

comes to the one

who backstabs

the most people,

thinking he is

"getting ahead".

Do you have
the guts
to achieve success
WITHOUT
stepping on others
to get ahead?

The most
egotistical
person is the one
who received
the most support
from people
he later refuses
to acknowledge
helped him
along the way.

Who has
reached back
to help you
and who
have you
reached back
to help?

The greatest eye
opener will happen
when a person who
thought he was so
"righteous" realizes he
is actually so far
behind the curve.

Is there such a thing
as being more righteous
than anyone else
outside of
Christ's sacrifice
of HIMSELF
on the cross?

The greatest
nightmare
is waking up
drowning
in the sea
of the afterlife
without the
eternal
Life Preserver.

If you
entered
the sea
of the
afterlife
today,
would you
sink or swim?

The most dangerous
person on earth
is the one
who bottles up
seething hatred
and spews all that
venom onto those least
deserving of it.

Do you know
a stranger
desperately in need
of a friend?

Could your
reaching out
<u>NOW</u> save lives?

The laziest man
on earth
is the one whose
daily planner
always begins with
tomorrow.

Who could you
help today
that could change
their tomorrow?

The most
peaceful soul
on earth
is the one
who has best come to
grips with the fact
that <u>everything</u> in
this life is foreknown
by the Creator.

Fulfill His thoughts
for you today by
choosing to walk in
love and peace
with others.

Did you know that
your Creator knows
everything that will
happen to you
throughout your
entire life?

Perhaps that is why
He constantly tells
His children that,
"Everything is going
to be alright."

The most problematic
person on earth
is the one
most passionate about
creating problems
for others.

Are you here
to create problems
for others

or are you
BLESSED
to solve problems
others cause?

The most passionate person to ever live is the <u>ONE</u> whose passion for us moved Him to suffer and die on the cross to become the bridge for us to get into Heaven.

Following Christ's
example,
for whom is your
passion leading
you to sacrifice?

The loneliest person
on earth is the one
who doesn't have even
herself as a true friend.

If today no one
on earth
accepts you,
accept yourself.

The person most
deceived is the one who
believes that causing
the most hurt somehow
helps the most people.

Hurting a woman
does not help her.

Hurting a man
does not help him.

Hurting children
does not help them.

Help people by LIFTING them
up, not putting them down.

છ૭ભ

THE PERSON WHO IS <u>ALWAYS</u> "ON THE GO" IS LIKELY LEAST CONTENT WITH HIMSELF.

છ૭ભ

DO YOU ALWAYS
WANT TO LEAVE
NO MATTER
WHERE YOU FIND
YOURSELF?

WHAT PRECIOUS
MOMENTS ARE
YOU MISSING?

•   •   •

Do you know what
your purpose is?

It is the <u>real</u> reason
that you were born
and it comes from
the One who
created you.

•   •   •

Those who stay committed to their predestined purpose enjoy the greatest inner peace. There is no greater fulfillment than doing what you were born to do in service to humanity.

• • •

The most admirable
people on earth are
those who pour out
love and support on
total strangers.

• • •

The heart that is empowered to love total strangers has captured a glimpse of heaven.

The most
unfulfilled person
is the one
who is furthest
from fulfilling
his purpose.

Do you want a
fulfilling life?
Pray to discover your
purpose and then
<u>pursue it</u> with every
fiber of your being.

The sweetest
person on earth
is also the
most thoughtful.

Did you know that
when you
heal the hurting,
Heaven celebrates
your act of kindness?

The greatest joy
comes from
worshipping in the
indescribable
presence of God.

During life's most
chaotic moments,
the value of
gut-wrenching
laughter cannot be
underestimated.

The most
courageous heart
sings joyfully during
the saddest
of times.

Most people are cheerful and pleasant when things are going well. But, true faith and courage compels us to rejoice during the worst times imaginable.

A soul filled
with the most
faith sees the
troubled sea as a
crosswalk.

Is the worst
storm in your
life <u>now</u> your
greatest
opportunity to
help others?

The "biggest loser" is the person who gained the most in this life but lost her soul somewhere along the way.

The greatest
winners in this life
are those willing to
risk fame and
fortune to help lost
sheep find their
Eternal Shepherd.

The scariest thought
is that your
greatest fear
will suddenly
become a reality.

But...

Faith
makes
fear
unwelcome.

The strongest person
on earth is the one
whose deep
compassion
lifts the
heaviest hearts.

Do you know
someone whose
heart is heavy with
sadness and grief?

How strong are you
because it's time
for some heavy
lifting…

The friendliest
person on earth
is the one
whose life mission
is to never meet
an *enemy*.

Imagine a world filled
only with friends who
are kind, loving and
thoughtful...and
WAIT...

...you're there leading
the pack.

Those boldest in sharing Christ's love often started as the most unlikely candidates.

What would change
if your faith
were as audacious
as the seed
of the giant
Sequoia tree?

The most narrow-minded person on earth is the one who ONLY drives down streets where the sign says "ONE WAY".

And it's their way
or the highway!

Have you
ever wondered
why God
didn't create
you first
and make
everyone else
your clone?

Celebrate Diversity

The most
forgiving
person on earth
is the one who
believes he has
been forgiven
the most.

If you want to be forgiven by your Maker for wrongs you have done - from your heart - you must forgive those who have wronged you.

The best teachers never cease to see themselves as students.

Life is learning.
Each day,
you are offered
a chance to learn
something new
that could
radically change
your circumstances.

• • •

THE MOST
CONFUSING
THEORY
SUGGESTS
THAT WHAT'S
MORALLY RIGHT
FOR YOU MAY
NOT BE MORALLY
RIGHT FOR ME.

A SOCIETY
THAT CANNOT
AGREE ON
BASIC MORALS
HAS
SENTENCED
ITSELF TO
ENDLESS
UNREST.

The biggest
blunder is to
assume that the
absence of
money makes
one "poor"
instead of the
absence of <u>love</u>.

True "riches" are
matters of the heart
– and the condition
of the soul –
not the contents of
your wallet.

The moment most

worthy of celebration

is strangely

the most ignored:

When you wake up

each morning and first

realize that

you're breathing.

Most things that
you think and do
after waking up,
are entirely
your choice.

But the choice of
whether or not you
wake up at all –
is God's alone.

The greatest rest
awaits the man
or woman who
worked tirelessly
helping others
find life
in Christ.

At the end
of each day,
rest well knowing that
you have selflessly
loved others without a
personal agenda that's
all about YOU…

… and you are not far
from the
Pearly Gates.

The biggest
"Drama King"
is the person
who causes the
MOST DRAMA
in the shortest
period of time.

There is a soap
opera where you
never want to be
a "character".

Don't choose to
star in your own
daytime drama!

The greatest deception is when a person makes so much effort to convince others of things that he <u>fully</u> knows are simply <u>not true</u>.

Honesty
BEGINS
the healing
process.

THE GREATEST
TRAGEDY IS
LIVING A FULL
LIFE WITHOUT
ONCE
CONSIDERING
WHAT WILL
HAPPEN AFTER
YOU - TAKE - YOUR
- LAST - BREATH.

So, where do you <u>honestly</u> believe you will be 60 seconds after you pass from this life?

The most
hardened heart
is the one so bitter,
angry, and unforgiving
that it resists
unconditional love
and fights those
only trying to help.

Do you know someone
whose heart is harder
than stone and whose
will is less flexible

than steel ?

If that person won't let
the Creator change
him, what are the odds
that you can?

The biggest
misunderstanding
is when the person
many consider to
be the most
"successful" dies
without Christ in
his heart.

True success
cannot enter
a room
where Christ
is uninvited.

*The most innocent person
on earth is the
adult whose
heart and faith
is most
childlike and pure.*

The person with the greatest faith believes that God can make what seems impossible – possible – <u>right now</u>.

The humblest person on earth sees himself as needing the most improvement, yet the most arrogant believes his sole purpose is to improve everyone else.

If humility and
arrogance were
two types of
hats, which
would you be
wearing today?

The most
<u>persistent</u> person
on earth is also
the most
<u>relentless</u> at
getting back up
and moving
forward.

A persistent spirit cannot be kept "in his proper place" as the only "place" for the persistent is <u>moving forward</u>.

THE MOST
LOVING PERSON
ON EARTH IS
THE ONE WHO
RECEIVED THE
LEAST AMOUNT
OF LOVE FROM
OTHERS, BUT
CHOSE TO LOVE
THE MOST.

THE <u>CHOICE</u> TO
FORGIVE AN
ABUSER SEEMS
IMPOSSIBLE, YET
ULTIMATELY IS
THE MOST
REWARDING ACT
OF COURAGE.

The person with the greatest faith views the most menacing thunderstorms of life as lullabies for a great night's sleep.

The greatest test is whether your faith in the Christ allows you to sleep <u>during</u> life's most perilous storms.

The most secure
person on earth is
not necessarily the
least jealous.

There is an aspect
of pure love
that is
(harmlessly) jealous
for the attention and
affection of its lover
and is justified.

The most talented
person on earth
is the one
who uses <u>one</u> ability
more effectively than
the person blessed
with <u>several</u> talents.

It's not what you have,
but how well you use
what you have, that
makes all
the difference.

The person with
the <u>purest</u> heart wakes up
every morning
with one thought:
"Who can I help today
that cannot possibly pay
me back?"

And...

If 10% of the world's population embraced selfless service, the power of that love would inspire a generation to stand up and fight for lasting peace, justice and prosperity for all willing to work for it.

The most selfless
person to ever live
ransomed His life
for those of us
who are the
<u>least</u> deserving.

Some have said, "only the strong survive." But, Christ taught us that those who are <u>truly</u> strong will use their strengths to help those who are <u>truly</u> hurting.

The most difficult
job on earth
is loving those
who interpret
acts of love
as acts of hate.

Love is like a
bulldozer
that doesn't
discriminate as it
moves forward with
purpose. It
intimidates hatred
wherever it finds it.

The person that is
the most
misguided risks
that which he
values most
for what
-in the end-
he values least.

Your choices reveal what you value and just how much you value what you value.

If you watched what you value on a large projector screen in front of all your friends and family, would you be proud or ashamed?

The best thing
to realize today
is that although
yesterday and
all prior days
have passed,
their potential
has not.

Past failures serve a
GREAT PURPOSE.

Through soul
searching,
HARD LESSONS
are learned,
BAD CYCLES
are broken,
and what was LOST
can now be FOUND
and REBIRTHED.

The "poorest of the poor" is the person richest in <u>potential</u> yet poorest in <u>production</u>.

It's not what's in
your bank and
investment accounts
that makes you rich,
but rather how
many lives you've
touched by
<u>selfless</u> acts
of kindness.

The "tallest" person
on earth is the one
who stoops the lowest
to help those
regarded as least
important.

You know you're "tall" <u>in your own eyes</u> when helping the poor feels like you have to "bend down" so low just to get to them.

People that occupy
the same home can
be the furthest apart.

And...

Only love
can bridge
the gap...

And...
love initiates.

The coldest nights are spent lying next to the person whose heart is so cold that you need a blanket just to lie next to him.

Love is gentle,
accepting, patient,
and…WARM.

The highest form of love
descended to
the lowest depth
to raise up those of us
who are
the least deserving.

Life's hidden
challenge is
recognizing the
"INVISIBLE" – those
all around us who are
silently screaming for
help while we giddily
rush by them
on our way
to get a latte.

The greatest truth is
the simplest yet
most difficult
for many to accept:

GOD ACTUALLY LOVES <u>EVERYONE</u>!

What would change if you tried your absolute best to think like your Creator and see OTHERS through unconditional eyes of LOVE?

Answer:

YOU

THE WORLD'S
WORST CRITIC WILL
ONE DAY FIND
HIMSELF THE MOST
CRITICIZED.

LOVE EVERYONE.

BE UNFAIRLY

CRITICAL OF

NO ONE.

The world's <u>most</u> annoying person is the one whose ego is so big that he can't fit his head through the door when he walks into a room.

If you are
suddenly stopped
at an invisible
door, it may be
because your

HUGE EGO

won't let you
enter.

The people
we will be
most thankful for
when we get to
Heaven are those who
encouraged us the
most in our faith
during the times we
thought of giving up.

The cost of giving up can be much greater than the present pain you're enduring.

Don't Give Up!

★ ★ ★ ★ ★ ★ ★ ★ ★ ★

The world's most generous person not only gives <u>the most</u> to support those considered "<u>the least</u>," but also mobilizes others to do the same.

★ ★ ★ ★ ★ ★ ★ ★ ★ ★

True generosity
involves
selfless sacrifices,
by those who can,
on behalf
of those who cannot.

The "dumbest" person is also the "smartest" person with the least respect for others.

Did you know
that kindness and
compassion are
expressions of
the highest form
of intelligence?

A troublemaking genius is far less useful than a peacemaker with below-average intellect.

The greatest travesty is when those with the highest "IQ" use their intelligence to stir up strife and disrupt peace, to carry out sinister plans.

The person
with the
most endurance
is often the one
who feels she has
the most to lose
by giving up.

Never discourage a person to give up on a dream that you did not put in her heart.

MOST INTERESTING
IS HOW SNAKES
ARE THE BEST
AT BLENDING IN,
BUT ARE THE LEAST
TRUSTWORTHY.

THE MOST DECEPTIVE PERSON CAN ALSO BE THE FRIENDLIEST!

The person that is the most bitter is also the most poisoned

...from within.

The very same
things that are
"wise" not to
forget are equally
"unwise" not
to forgive.

The hungriest
person on earth
is also the least
satisfied.

• • •

The relationships many
<u>recklessly</u> crave
are often the
least satisfying.

• • •

The angriest person
is also the one
most blinded by
his own rage.

True love
holds tight
enough to rescue
yet loose enough
to release.

THE LONELIEST
PERSON IS OFTEN
SURROUNDED BY
THE MOST
SO-CALLED
"FRIENDS".

LIKE CLOUDS
BUILDING A
TOWER OF
PRAISE IN THE
SKY, JUST AS
QUICKLY AS FAN
CLUBS FORM TO
"FOLLOW" YOU,
THEY CAN
SCATTER IN A
STRONG WIND
OF GOSSIP.

THE PERSON THAT IS THE MOST MISERABLE IS OFTEN THE MOST SELF-CENTERED.

THE INFLATION OF "SELF" IS THE DEFLATION OF HAPPINESS.

The person most
addicted to
curiosity is not
found except at
the next party.

The soul with an
insatiable desire for
wild parties has the
least inner peace.

The greatest
paradox is that
many "rich" people
are "poor" in
helping others and
many "poor" people
are "rich" in
generosity.

Give to others as if TODAY were your last day on earth and TOMORROW your life review begins before the Eternal Judge, who shows partiality to no one.

. . .

The greatest rewards
will go to those who
showed the most
compassion when it
was least convenient.

. . .

If there is something you
feel compelled to do
to help people,
but you refrain because
it seems "so inconvenient,"
don't worry because
your reward
can find a new home
with the person doing what
God originally
called YOU to do.

Even the closest of
friends can quickly
become estranged
after the gossiper
shows up to divide
and conquer.

Those most masterful in
manipulation continuously
resort to the following
psychological tactics:
1. Lies
2. Intimidation
3. Guilt

If those schemes do not force
their victim into submission,
they may resort to physical
violence and isolate their victim
so no one notices the bruises.

THE HEAVIEST
WEIGHT IS
CARRIED BY THE
PERSON
VINDICATED IN
THE EYES OF THE
PUBLIC, BUT
CONVICTED IN
HIS OWN HEART.

IT IS NOT THOSE WHOM MAN VINDICATES — BUT WHOM GOD VINDICATES — THAT ARE TRULY FREE.

Your best
friend could
strangely be
the person
with whom
you agree
<u>the least</u>.

Sometimes God sends people to challenge us when He sees we are beginning to settle for less than His best.

The biggest idol is
found in the heart
of the person who is
the most controlling.

The only One who
has the right to
dictate how we are to
live our lives is God.

**In Heaven,
the most
"frequent flier"
will not
be the person who
accumulated
the most
air miles,
but the one
who traveled the
most in selfless
service to others.**

How much do accolades really matter if we cannot carry our plaques and awards with us into eternity?

The eyes
of the <u>GREEDY</u>
light up far more
when hearing
about how
much <u>MONEY</u>
they earned than
how many people
they helped.

"Bankruptcy"
has been filed
in the soul
of the person
whose <u>every</u> thought is
"Show me the money!"

THE GREATEST TEACHERS ARE OFTEN THE QUIET ONES WHO LEAD BY EXAMPLE.

THE PERSON WHO IS NOT LEADING BY EXAMPLE IS NOT LEADING AT ALL.

The most
celebrated soul in
Heaven is the one
who most
celebrated others
while she
herself was
celebrated least.

It would take an explosion of LOVE to make "selfless service" go viral.

The most impactful
invention is the one
without which we
cannot live.

We can live without the latest gadget, but who can say that they were TRULY ALIVE that never learned how to LOVE?

The most
forgiving is
the one who
<u>most</u> realizes
just how much
she has been
forgiven.

When we truly realize how much we've been forgiven through the cross, we are empowered to <u>forgive without limits</u>.

Isn't it odd that
the person most
spoiled by others
is often the
<u>least</u> generous?

• • •

Anyone can master
receiving, but it takes
love to master
selfless giving.

When we give
selflessly, only
Heaven knows the
full extent of our
sacrifices for others.

Does your family know how much you love them by how you treat THEM or how they see you treat OTHERS?

And. . .

If your "charity
BEGINS at home,"
then where does it go
after you leave
the house?

The most responsible person is also the most reliable.

Doubtful a person will be
called these virtues in
Heaven if never on earth:

Trustworthy,
Faithful,
Genuine.

Faith, without
corresponding action,
has no significance.

The person most prepared to lead is often the most content to continue following a leader.

In life, most of the real action happens behind the scenes.

The most educated
is the one who uses
her knowledge,
training and
experience to
empower others.

To what degree
does your education
and knowledge
benefit the least
fortunate members
of society?

• • •

The heavier
your cross, the
lighter your
soul.

Don't shirk responsibility! If you're always "the one giving," then in Heaven, you'll be forever receiving. Pay it forward.

Do you know anyone whose soul seems to be filled with darkness, despair and depression? What is the BEST way to show him compassion right now?

Answer:

Give him the BEST NEWS, that there is a cure for his condition - a Supernatural Love just waiting to flood his dark soul with an Eternal Light that never goes out.

The greatest cure for the darkest soul came at the greatest price:

The cross of Christ.

Prayer For Eternal Life

I am very excited that somehow this thought-provoking and inspiring material found its way to you. If you already have a relationship with Christ, that's wonderful! If not, and you're ready to live life with higher purpose, start today by inviting Christ into your heart by praying this simple prayer:

Father and Creator of Heaven and earth, thank you for giving me life and for protecting me all the way up until this very moment. I recognize that I have failed to live my life in a perfect way and that I cannot offer you anything worth the value of my soul. That's why you sent Jesus Christ to die on the cross for me.

Father, forgive me of my sins and break the powers of darkness in my life through the authority of your Son, Jesus Christ.
I give you my heart, body and soul to keep for all eternity. Help me to live the rest of my life serving you by helping others.

Amen.

Superlatives from Heaven

The photograph above depicts some of the
orphans and other children that
Mr. Parker and his team supports at the
Blanchard Orphanage,
in Croix Des Bouquets, Haiti.

Superlatives from Heaven

GPM's Selfless Service Missionary Spotlight

Let's reprioritize our busy lives and give honor to whom honor is due, especially those who epitomize the spirit of selfless service, such as Guerry and Gerda LeFranc of Zamar Ministries, in Haiti.

In partnership with Global Parallel Ministries, Inc. (GPM), Zamar Ministries distributes food, clothing, supplies and clean drinkable water to the underprivileged residents of Croix Des Bouquets, Haiti. Zamar Ministries also operates a mobile medical clinic for the poor in urban and rural areas in Haiti.

Above is a photograph of a private school operated by Zamar Ministries in Haiti.
To plan a mission trip to help the hurting in Haiti, please email the author at Starr@globalparallel.com

globalparallel.com

www.ingramcontent.com/pod-product-compliance
Lightning Source LLC
Chambersburg PA
CBHW072000040426
42447CB00009B/1413